Identifying the Obstacles to High-Impact Entrepreneurship in Latin America and the Caribbean

Zoltan J. Acs, George Mason University

Paulo Correa, World Bank

This paper was produced with support from the Innovation Policy Platform
(www.innovationpolicyplatform.org).

Contents

About the authors...iii
Acknowledgments.. **Error! Bookmark not defined.**
Using the Global Entrepreneurship Development Index (GEDI) to measure high-impact
entrepreneurship..1
   From the individual to the system: Shifting policy paradigms on entrepreneurship 2
     Entrepreneurship theory: The limits of the existing body of knowledge 3
     The challenge of effectively measuring entrepreneurship at the country level 4
   A new concept: The national system of entrepreneurship 5
What the GEDI says about entrepreneurship in Latin America...7
   GEDI results for efficiency-driven economies...8
   GEDI results in factor-driven economies 10
The potential for high-impact entrepreneurship in Latin America: Case study evidence.........................11
   The following sections provide an overview of the most salient characteristics of each
   case study, based on the six main themes presented earlier..13
   What types of innovations are high-impact entrepreneurs developing in Latin America?.....................13
   How are high-impact companies financed at the early stages of development? 17
   How does the availability of qualified human capital contribute to high-impact
   entrepreneurship? 18
   What role do globalization and international networks play in the development of
   high-impact companies?..19
   How do government action and culture influence high-impact entrepreneurship? 21
   What role do personal and professional networks play in supporting high-impact
   entrepreneurial activity? 23
Conclusion: Policy themes 24
References 27
Appendix 1. The individual variables used in the GEDI...30
Appendix 2. Description and sources for the institutional variables used in the GEDI 31

Figures

Figure 1. Structure of GEDI: from variables to subindexes...7
Figure 2. Comparisons of factor-driven and efficiency-driven countries in Latin America on the GEDI 8
Figure 3. Comparative performance on the GEDI of efficiency-driven countries in Europe, Asia, and Latin
America 9
Figure 4. Comparative performance on the GEDI of large and small efficiency-driven countries in Latin
America 10
Figure 5. Comparative performance on the GEDI of factor-driven countries in the Middle East and North
Africa, Asia, and Latin America 11

Tables

Table 1. Characteristics of nine cases of successful entrepreneurship in Latin America 12
Table 2. The relative Importance of six main themes to case study companies 13
Table 3. Funding sources for the creation of seven firms profiled in this study 18

About the Authors

Zoltan J. Ac, Ph.D is a Professorial Fellow at The London School of Economics and University Professor at George Mason University. He is the leading advocate of the importance of entrepreneurship for economic development. Along with Dr. Laszlo Szerb he is the founder of the Global Entrepreneurship and Development Index (GEDI) that is the first tool to track entrepreneurship and economic development in the global economy. He received the 2001 International Award for Entrepreneurship and Small Business Research, on behalf of The Swedish National Board for Industrial and Technical Development. His most recent book Why Philanthropy Matters: How the Wealthy Give, and What It Means for Our Economic Well-Being, 2013, was published by Princeton University Press.

Paulo Correa is a Lead Economist at the Trade and Competitiveness Global Practice of the World Bank Group. He joined the Bank in 2002 from the Ministry of Finance, Brazil. Mr. Correa has led a number of projects and studies in the areas of innovation, competition, and trade and competitiveness, including more recently the Croatia Science and Technology Project (2006-2011); the Western Balkans R&D for Innovation Regional Strategy Technical Assistance Project (2012-2013); the Russia's Export Diversification through Competition and Innovation Report (2012); and Turkey's National Innovation System Assessment (2009). He holds a M.Sc. in Economics from the University of Western Ontario and a M.Sc. in Industrial Economics from the Federal University of Rio de Janeiro. He has published more recently in the World Bank Economic Review; the Journal of International Trade and Economic Development; and the Quarterly Review of Economics and Finance.

Acknowledgements

The authors thank Carlos Hinojosa (carlos.hinojosa@technopolis-group.com) for his contributions to this paper. The case studies were conducted by Ruta Aidis (raidis@hotmail.com), Adriana Kocornik-Mina (akocornik@gmail.com), and David Miller (dmillerq@gmu.edu). The authors also want to thank Xavier Cirera, Esperanza Lasagabaster, Daniel Lederman, Marialisa Motta and Jamele Rigolini for their valuable comments to previous versions of the paper.

High-impact companies are a very important source of economic and job growth. Identifying the drivers and barriers behind their development is key to developing a sound supporting policy framework. The Global Entrepreneurship Development Index (GEDI) can interpret and measure entrepreneurial capacity as a systemic phenomenon. For that reason it provides a powerful means of assessing regional entrepreneurial performance.

This paper begins by analyzing GEDI results in order to draw a picture of how well entrepreneurship systems perform in Latin America and the Caribbean (LAC). The lessons drawn from this analysis are deepened through the qualitative analysis of nine case studies on the creation and development of successful high-impact companies in the region.

The paper has four main sections. The first presents GEDI and distinguishes it from traditional approaches to measuring entrepreneurship. The second looks at GEDI results for LAC countries and compares them to other groups of countries around the world. The third present the evidence drawn from case studies, showcasing nine high-impact companies in the region. The last section provides general conclusions as well as some elements for reflection for policymakers seeking to support the development of high-impact entrepreneurship.

Using the Global Entrepreneurship Development Index (GEDI) to measure high-impact entrepreneurship

High-impact companies and high-impact entrepreneurship can be defined in several ways. Generally, high-impact entrepreneurship is defined as a phase of growth in a business organization characterized by very rapid rates of revenue and employment growth over a certain time period. For example, the U.S. Small Business Administration defines high impact companies as "enterprises whose sales have at least doubled over a four-year period and which have an employment growth quantifier of two or more over the same period." High-impact companies tend to be highly adaptable and appear to be resilient to the changes generated by business cycles. They can be found in all sectors and tend to be leaders in their sectors. High growth constitutes a phase in firm growth and is not restricted to any particular type of firm (OECD 2010). As such, high-growth companies are not necessarily start-ups but are generally created by two or three founders. They generally exhibit low concentrations of managerial activity.

High-impact companies are a very important source of net job creation even though they represent a small proportion of the business population (OECD 2010). In advanced economies such as the United States, these business outliers represent only 2–4 percent of all firms, but their capacity to generate employment makes them key to economic and social growth and development.

In addition to their capacity to spur employment, high-impact companies and entrepreneurs as understood in this paper have a transformative nature. This includes the capacity "to create or carry on an enterprise where not all the markets are well established or clearly defined and/or in which the relevant parts of the production function are not completely known" (Leibenstein 1978). In addition, in a developing country context, such companies grow far beyond the scope of an individual's subsistence needs and generate positive effects at the community level (Schoar 2009). The case studies presented in the later sections of this paper illustrate the transformative nature of high-impact companies, whether it be by improving living conditions in local communities or creating new markets.

Identifying and measuring the drivers and indicators linked to the successful creation of high-impact companies poses significant challenges. It requires developing a combined approach based on both the economic theory of the firm as a collective actor and the theory of entrepreneurship, focusing on the work of an individual or group of individuals. The GEDI was specifically designed to track the factors leading to the creation of high-impact firms in different countries. While the method of the GEDI builds on ideas developed in the literature on national innovation systems (NIS) and other entrepreneurship research, it has one key distinguishing feature: It combines individual and institutional variables, while considering the interdependencies of the system. This reflects the notion that framework conditions (institutions and linkages) influence the kinds of incentives that individual agents must pursue, as well as the economic and social opportunities accessible through entrepreneurial activity.

GEDI is the first complex index to focus on the multidimensional quality rather than the quantitative aspects of entrepreneurship. By reducing several variables to essentially one, this composite index provides useful summary information about the multidimensional phenomena behind entrepreneurship and firm growth. To reflect the interdependent nature of indicators, GEDI is based on a "penalty for bottleneck" (PFB) methodology, the central tenet of which is that the performance of the system depends on the weakest link. Higher-scoring indicators cannot exhibit their full effect on the performance of the system because of the bottleneck. The uniqueness of this methodology is that the elements of the system are only partially substitutable for one another.

Use of the PFB methodology can influence policymaking because it can identify the weakest link in a country, both at the institutional and individual levels, thus highlighting particular policy needs. GEDI can also be used to track changes over time to assess the impact of policy changes. The index relies on two types of data sources: (i) the institutional data originating from internationally recognized, publicly available data sources, such as the Global Competitiveness Report, the Index of Economic Freedom, the World Bank's Ease of Doing Business index, the United Nations, the United Nations Educational, Scientific, and Cultural Organization (UNESCO), and the KOF Index of Globalization; and (ii) the data on individuals from the Global Entrepreneurship Monitor's (GEM) world survey.

While the index can be relied on to identify a particular country's strengths and weaknesses, it does not provide insight into how firms overcome those weaknesses or benefit from those strengths. To better gauge the challenges faced by high-impact entrepreneurs, this discussion complements GEDI's statistically based analysis with case studies from nine Latin American countries.[1] The cases cover a range of industries and firms, from a high-end software development company in Argentina to hair salons using a revolutionary approach in Brazil. The cases are developed along six main themes: innovation, finance, globalization, human capital, culture, and networking. These six themes are similar to the 15 pillars of GEDI. GEDI measures these six themes and nine others. The case study highlights that perhaps some pillars in GEDI are more important than others.

From the individual to the system: Shifting policy paradigms on entrepreneurship

The following section provides an overview of the traditional approaches to entrepreneurship measurement and their recent development. It goes on to explain the approach developed by the GEDI, which is based on calculating the performance of "national entrepreneurship systems," taking into account the individual and collective/institutional dimensions of entrepreneurship activity.

---

[1] The case studies were conducted by Ruta Aidis (raidis@hotmail.com), Adriana Kocornik-Mina (akocornik@gmail.com), and David Miller (dmillerq@gmu.edu). The full text of the case studies is available from zacs@gmu.edu.

Entrepreneurship theory: The limits of the existing body of knowledge

Surprising as it may sound, explicit focus on entrepreneurship is a relatively recent development in the policy world. Although David Birch (1979) first reported on the importance of new firms to job creation in the late 1970s, the data that make it possible to measure this relationship across countries did not emerge until 10 to 15 years ago.[2] The first test round of what was called the Global Entrepreneurship Monitor took place in 1998 (Reynolds, Bosma, and Autio 2005), while the World Bank's Ease of Doing Business index was launched in late 2001. The Organisation for Economic Co-operation and Development (OECD) began tracking entrepreneurship policies in the mid-2000s (Hoffmann, Larsen, and Oxholm 2006). Because most efforts to track entrepreneurship began relatively recently, the understanding of harnessing it for economic growth is still evolving.

This is not to deny that much has been learned. Among the major insights gleaned from research over the past 15 years have been the shift in focus from new firms to "gazelles" as sources of job creation (Autio 2007; Birch, Haggerty, and Parsons 1997); the recognition of the importance of small firms in innovation and the subsequent understanding of the role of new firms in facilitating the economic exploitation of knowledge generated by research (Acs et al. 2009; Audretsch and Keilbach 2008); and the recognition that entrepreneurship may mean very different things at different stages of economic development (Bosma et al. 2009). But while the role of entrepreneurship in economic development has gradually become clearer, little is known about the policies that can be used to harness its potential. This is mostly because of insufficient understanding of the entrepreneurial agency of individuals in the NIS literature (Radosevic 2007) and the lack of appreciation for contextual influences in the entrepreneurship literature (Acs, Autio, and Szerb 2014).

To date, the main approach to exploring innovation and entrepreneurship in economic systems has built on the NIS emphasis on the role of institutions in the generation and dissemination of knowledge (Freeman 1988; Lundvall 1992; Nelson 1993), while individual-level entrepreneurial agency is either not considered or is assumed to occur automatically (Radosevic 2007). In the NIS literature, institutions engender, regulate, and reinforce individual action. This routine-reinforcing perspective has not been reconciled with the individual-centered, routine-breaking emphasis of the entrepreneurship literature (Radosevic 2007; Schmid 2004).

In contrast to the systemic emphasis of the NIS literature, research on entrepreneurship has centered almost exclusively on the individual (or team), and most often on the connection between the individual and opportunity (Shane and Venkataraman 2000). In the dominant (Austrian) portrayal individuals react to opportunities: Central to the entrepreneurial process is whether opportunities exist and whether individuals are sufficiently alert to recognize and act upon them (Kirzner 1973, 1997). Consequently, much effort has gone into understanding what enables some individuals to recognize and pursue opportunities successfully. Either opportunities have been seen as being produced by outside individuals, or individuals have been considered to be creating their own (Alvarez and Barney 2007). Beyond examining the entrepreneur's immediate context (for example, social networks), this research has not systematically explored the links between the entrepreneur and the wider economic system.

---

[2] There were earlier initiatives, such as the Observatory of European SMEs, which began surveying small and medium-sized enterprises in 1992. Harmonized cross-country data on new firm creation did not begin to emerge until later, however.

The gap between the focus of the NIS literature, which overlooks entrepreneurial agency, and entrepreneurship research, which ignores the individual's wider context, gives rise to two kinds of fallacies, which are reflected in current efforts to measure entrepreneurship in countries.

The "ecological fallacy" assumes that attributes at the group level are directly reflected in the attitudes, aspirations, and abilities of the individual (Javidan et al. 2006; Robinson 1950; Seligson 2002). An example of the ecological fallacy would be the assumption that all that is needed to understand the entrepreneurial character of a given country is to study its entrepreneurial framework—its institutions, policies, policy programs, support structures, infrastructure, and incentive systems. In this line of thinking, individual-level data are not needed because the country's framework conditions are assumed to define individual action.

By contrast, the "individualistic fallacy" is the assumption that countries are king-sized individuals (Hofstede 2001, 21; Seligson 2002, 273). This fallacy is implicit in the aggregation of individual-level attitudes, abilities, and aspirations to the level of the entire national economy. The Individualistic fallacy would be reflected in the assumption that all that is needed to describe a country's capacity for entrepreneurship are national aggregates of individual-level attitudes, abilities, and aspirations. Here, the implicit assumption is that social systems obey the same behavioral logic and respond to incentives as individuals do. In other words, the individualistic fallacy assumes wider social systems do not exhibit any characteristics distinct from those of individuals.

The challenge of effectively measuring entrepreneurship at the country level

Both the "ecological" and "individualistic" fallacies are reflected in current attempts to measure entrepreneurship in countries. In particular, ecological assumptions can be detected in the "framework measures" of country-level entrepreneurship (Acs et al. 2012). Three types of framework measures exist. One approach surveys national experts to construct multi-item scales that reflect entrepreneurial framework conditions (see, for example, Coduras and Autio 2012; Reynolds et al. 2005); another characterizes the national regulatory framework for new business entry (Djankov et al. 2002). A good example of the latter is the World Bank's Ease of Doing Business index. Building, in part, on this index, the OECD Entrepreneurship Indicators Program has developed a more comprehensive framework measure that distinguishes among framework conditions, entrepreneurship performance, and economic impact (Ahmad and Hoffmann 2008).

Such indicators provide very useful benchmarks of the institutional, policy, and regulatory frameworks for entrepreneurship in a country. But although they are invaluable for policy benchmarking and monitoring, they do not provide insight into how individuals interact with their systemic contexts.

A third group of measures tracks the incidence of new firms or self-employment entries within a population. In these indicators, "entrepreneurship" is conceived of as the creation of a new business organization or an entry into self-employment. Population-level aggregates of activities and attitudes (or, alternatively, density measures) are then used to describe a country's entrepreneurial character. Examples of such "output" indicators include: the Global Entrepreneurship Monitor's Total Entrepreneurial Activity (TEA) index (Reynolds and others 2005); the OECD-Eurostat's Entrepreneurship Indicators Program (which also tracks firm creations; see, for example, Lunati, Meyer zu Schlochtern, and Sargsayan 2010; OECD-Eurostat 2007); the World Bank's Entrepreneurship Survey (2011); and the Flash Eurobarometer survey (Gallup 2009). Examples of indexes measuring population-level attitudes include the Eurobarometer survey (Gallup 2009); the World Values Survey; the Global Entrepreneurship Monitor (GEM); and the International Social Survey (ISSP 1997).

Like framework indicators, output indicators offer many benefits, most obviously the ability to track entrepreneurial entries and attitudes. There are two types. Registry-based measures track formal entries, while survey-based measures track overall entries.[3] Both approaches, however, exhibit the individualistic fallacy by ignoring the context in which entrepreneurial entries occur. As a result, they imply that entries have the same impact regardless of context—that is, that the context does not meaningfully regulate the relationship between action and outcomes.

A new concept: The national system of entrepreneurship

Both framework and output indicators of entrepreneurship have their merits. The susceptibility of each to the aforementioned fallacies presents challenges, however, when profiling national systems of entrepreneurship. As a result, no measure properly embeds individual-level attitudes, abilities, and aspirations within a wider systemic context. In reality, of course, both institutions and individuals matter. If individuals do not act, entrepreneurship will not happen, no matter how perfect the institutional framework. On the other hand, individual action will not generate much impact in the absence of an appropriate institutional framework. A high-technology start-up, for example, will have much greater economic potential in Silicon Valley than in Uganda even if its intrinsic quality is the same.

The GEDI method resolves this dilemma by adopting an approach based on the notion of the national system of entrepreneurship (Acs et al. 2012). This approach is based on five premises:

- Entrepreneurship is fundamentally individual-level action (that is, undertaken and driven by individuals).

- This action mobilizes resources to pursue opportunities through the creation of new firms.

- Action is mediated by complex interactions of attitudes, abilities, and activities at the level of the society or culture.

- Action occurs within a multifaceted economic, social, and institutional context.

- This dynamic drives economic productivity through the allocation of resources to efficient uses.

Consequently, the GEDI adopts the following definition of national systems of entrepreneurship:

> *A national system of entrepreneurship is the dynamic, institutionally embedded interaction of the entrepreneurial attitudes, abilities, and aspirations of individuals, which drives the allocation of resources through the creation and operation of new ventures.*

The GEDI methodology approaches country-level entrepreneurship as a systemic phenomenon that is driven by the interaction between entrepreneurial individuals and system-level framework conditions, which it captures by the way it profiles countries. Systemic features of national systems of innovation are captured by GEDI's (i) contextualization of individual-level data, by weighting them with data describing a country's framework conditions; (ii) use of 15 context-weighted pillars of entrepreneurial attitudes, abilities, and aspirations, which are further organized into three subindexes (described

---

[3] Currently, no index exists to track informal entries.

below); (iii) recognition that several pillars combine to produce system-level performance; and (iv) consequent recognition that national entrepreneurial performance may be held back by *bottleneck factors* (that is, poorly performing pillars that may constrain system performance).

The GEDI begins by weighing 15 individual variables with a corresponding set of institutional variables. The resulting set of pillars is categorized into three entrepreneurship subindexes[4]:

- *Entrepreneurial attitudes* are attitudes associated with the entrepreneurship-related behavior of a country's population, including opportunity perception, skills, risk aversion, networking potential, and cultural support.

- *Entrepreneurial ability* is principally concerned with the potential of owners of nascent and start-up businesses to produce high growth, which is assessed using measures of quality, activity in a technology-intensive sector, level of education, and the uniqueness of the offered product or service in relationship to those of competitors.

- *Entrepreneurial aspiration* refers to distinctive, qualitative, market-expanding, wealth-enhancing entrepreneurial activity, as reflected in the newness of the product and the technology a venture uses, internationalization, high-growth ambitions, and the availability of risk capital.

Figure 1 presents an overview of the GEDI indicators, focusing on individual and institutional variables. Detailed descriptions of these indicators and the associated sources of data are presented in appendixes 1 and 2.

---

[4] The 19 indicators presented in appendix 1 are reduced to 15 variables in GEDI. This is because several indicators are combined to form a single variable.

Figure 1. Structure of GEDI: from variables to subindexes

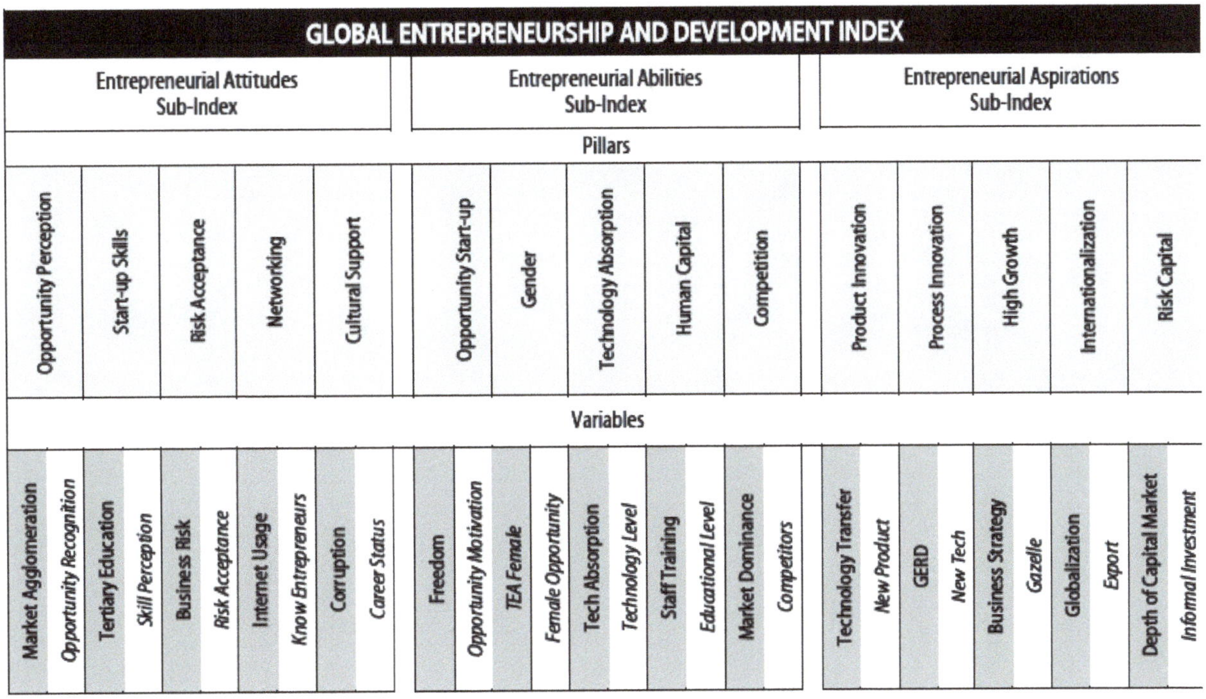

GLOBAL ENTREPRENEURSHIP AND DEVELOPMENT INDEX		
Entrepreneurial Attitudes Sub-Index	Entrepreneurial Abilities Sub-Index	Entrepreneurial Aspirations Sub-Index
Pillars		
Opportunity Perception / Start-up Skills / Risk Acceptance / Networking / Cultural Support	Opportunity Start-up / Gender / Technology Absorption / Human Capital / Competition	Product Innovation / Process Innovation / High Growth / Internationalization / Risk Capital
Variables		
Market Agglomeration / Opportunity Recognition / Tertiary Education / Skill Perception / Business Risk / Risk Acceptance / Internet Usage / Know Entrepreneurs / Corruption / Career Status	Freedom / Opportunity Motivation / TEA Female / Female Opportunity / Tech Absorption / Technology Level / Staff Training / Educational Level / Market Dominance / Competitors	Technology Transfer / New Product / GERD / New Tech / Business Strategy / Gazelle / Globalization / Export / Depth of Capital Market / Informal Investment

Source: ACS et al. 2013, p. 217.

By capturing system dynamics, the GEDI goes beyond traditional, linear-additive index approaches (as discussed below). Fundamental to the concept of national systems of entrepreneurship is the notion that (i) systems, by definition, comprise multiple components; and (ii) these components interact to produce system-level performance. These are defining characteristics of any system that linear-additive indexes fail to capture. In a linear-additive index, the overall index value is merely the sum of the values of individual components. This implies that each component contributes directly and independently to system performance. In the context of entrepreneurship, this would mean, for example, that a national measure of education would contribute directly (independently of other system components) to "national entrepreneurship." In reality, we know that education cannot contribute much to a country's entrepreneurial performance if individuals fail to act. On the other hand, without education, the economic potential of entrepreneurial entries would be severely constrained. Even with both education and entrepreneurial action, country-level entrepreneurial performance would be constrained by a lack of growth aspirations or financial resources to foster the growth of new ventures. A linear-additive index would fail to recognize such interactions, thereby ignoring crucial aspects of system-level performance.

What the GEDI says about entrepreneurship in Latin America

An analysis of cross-regional and intraregional GEDI results sheds light on some of the main trends found within entrepreneurship systems, helping us identify roadblocks to and drivers behind the development of high-impact companies. Because development levels among Latin American countries contrast greatly, we divide the analysis of the GEDI results into two sections: one on factor-driven countries and one on efficiency-driven countries.[5] The sharp differences between the two groups of countries are illustrated in figure 2, which displays the relative performance of both groups of countries for each pillar of the GEDI. The figure shows that efficiency-driven economies outperform factor-driven economies on every pillar, except for start-up skills and gender. Low levels of process innovation, however, appear as a common trait of both groups of countries.

Figure 2. Comparisons of factor-driven and efficiency-driven countries in Latin America on the GEDI

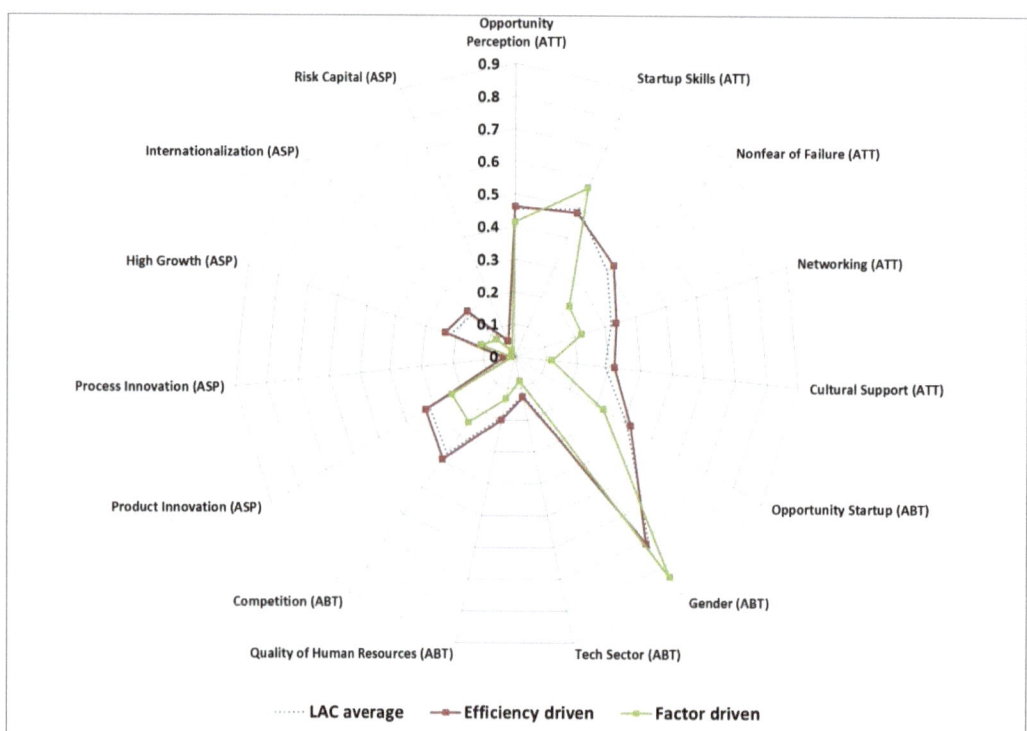

Source: Acs, Szerb, and Autio 2013.
Note: In this spidergram, 0.90 is the maximum value. GEDI pillars are assessed on a scale from 0 to 1.
ASP = aspirations, ABT = ability, ATT= attitudes.
Efficiency-driven: Argentina, Barbados, Belize, Brazil, Chile, Colombia, Costa Rica, Dominican Republic, Ecuador, El Salvador, Guatemala, Jamaica, Mexico, Panama, Paraguay, Peru, Uruguay.
Factor-driven: Bolivia, Honduras, Venezuela.

GEDI results for efficiency-driven economies

Figure 3 illustrates the comparative performance of efficiency-driven countries in Latin America, Europe, and Asia based on GEDI results. The figure illustrates each region's position in comparison to the other two individually, as well as in comparison to the average for the three groups. A breakdown for each of the index's pillars and subindexes (attitudes, abilities, and aspirations) is also provided.

---

[5] According to the World Economic Forum's Global Competitiveness Report, factor-driven economies compete based on their factor endowments—primarily unskilled labor and natural resources. As a country becomes more competitive, productivity will increase and wages will rise with advancing development. Countries will then move into the efficiency-driven stage of development, where they must begin to develop more-efficient production processes and increase product quality because wages have risen and prices cannot be raised.

Figure 3. Comparative performance on the GEDI of efficiency-driven countries in Europe, Asia, and Latin America

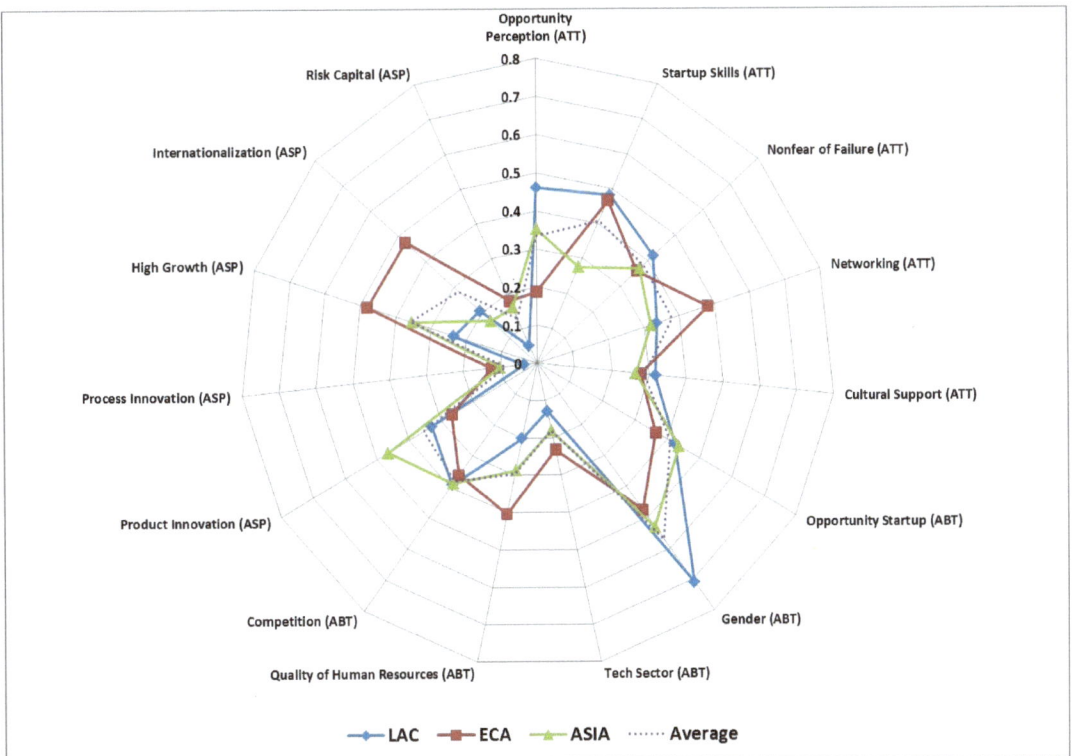

Source: Acs, Szerb, and Autio 2013.

Note: In this spidergram, 0.80 is the maximum value. GEDI pillars are assessed on a scale from 0 to 1.

ASP = aspirations, ABT = ability, ATT= attitudes

Efficiency-driven Central European and Asian countries (ECA): Albania, Bosnia and Herzegovina, Bulgaria, Croatia, Estonia, Hungary, Kazakhstan, Latvia, Lithuania, Poland, Romania, Russia, Serbia, Slovakia, Ukraine, Macedonia, Montenegro.

Efficiency-driven Asian countries: China, Indonesia, Malaysia, Thailand, Turkey.

Efficiency-driven Latin Amercia countries (LAC): Argentina, Barbados, Belize, Brazil, Chile, Colombia, Costa Rica, Dominican Republic, Ecuador, El Salvador, Guatemala, Jamaica, Mexico, Panama, Paraguay, Peru, Uruguay.

This information permits several observations regarding the entrepreneurship performance of efficiency-driven Latin American economies:

- Latin American efficiency-driven economies outperform their Asian and European counterparts on four of GEDI's pillars: gender, opportunity perception, non-fear of failure, and cultural support (all of which fall under the attitudes index). They fall significantly short, however, in terms of product and process innovation, quality of human resources, high growth aspirations, and risk capital. While LAC seems to perform well in terms of entrepreneurship attitudes, it significantly underperforms on pillars under the aspirations subindex.

- All three sets of countries exhibit similarities in terms of start-up skills and competition.

- The three sets of countries differ significantly in entrepreneurial aspirations and desire to build high-impact companies. Europe and Asia both outperform Latin America on process innovation, high-growth aspirations, and risk capital. Notably, European countries significantly outperform both Asia and Latin America on high-growth aspirations and internationalization. On high-growth companies and internationalization, for example, Latin America falls more than 30 points behind Europe.

The comparison of a group of large and small efficiency-driven LAC countries demonstrates that smaller countries slightly outperform larger ones. Figure 4 displays GEDI averages for Mexico, Argentina, and Brazil, on the one hand; and Uruguay, Panama, and Costa Rica, on the other. The group of smaller countries obtains higher scores on all entrepreneurial attitudes pillars but one (opportunity perception), as well as on competition, product innovation, internationalization, and risk capital. Higher population size does not appear to drive levels of performance in national entrepreneurship systems.

Figure 4. Comparative performance on the GEDI of large and small efficiency-driven countries in Latin America

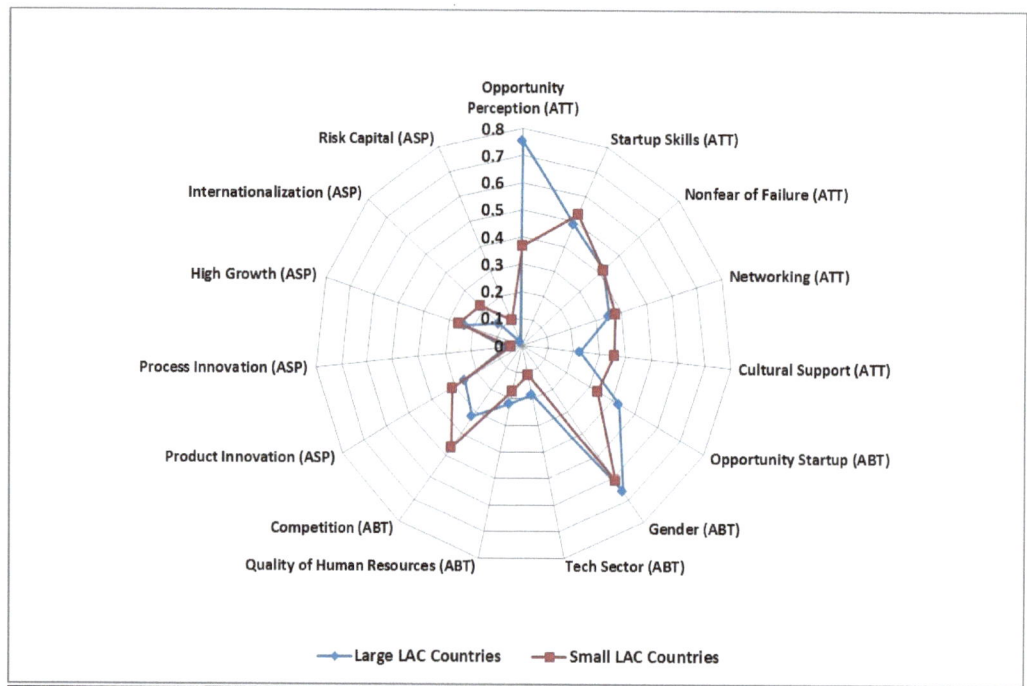

Source: Acs, Szerb, and Autio 2013.
Note: In this spidergram, 0.80 is the maximum value. GEDI pillars are assessed on a scale from 0 to 1.
ASP = aspirations, ABT = ability, ATT= attitudes.
Large LAC countries = Mexico, Argentina, and Brazil.
Small LAC countries = Uruguay, Panama, and Costa Rica.

GEDI results in factor-driven economies

The analysis of GEDI results in factor-driven economies in LAC, the Middle East and North Africa (MENA), and Asia brings forth a number of common trends. Factor-driven countries are characterized by low levels of entrepreneurial aspirations, particularly risk capital, process innovation, tech sector development, and internationalization. On the other hand, these countries tend to perform well in entrepreneurial attitude–related fields, such as opportunity perception and networking. Factor-driven countries in MENA perform better than their Asian and Latin American counterparts on the majority of GEDI pillars.

Figure 5. Comparative performance on the GEDI of factor-driven countries in the Middle East and North Africa, Asia, and Latin America

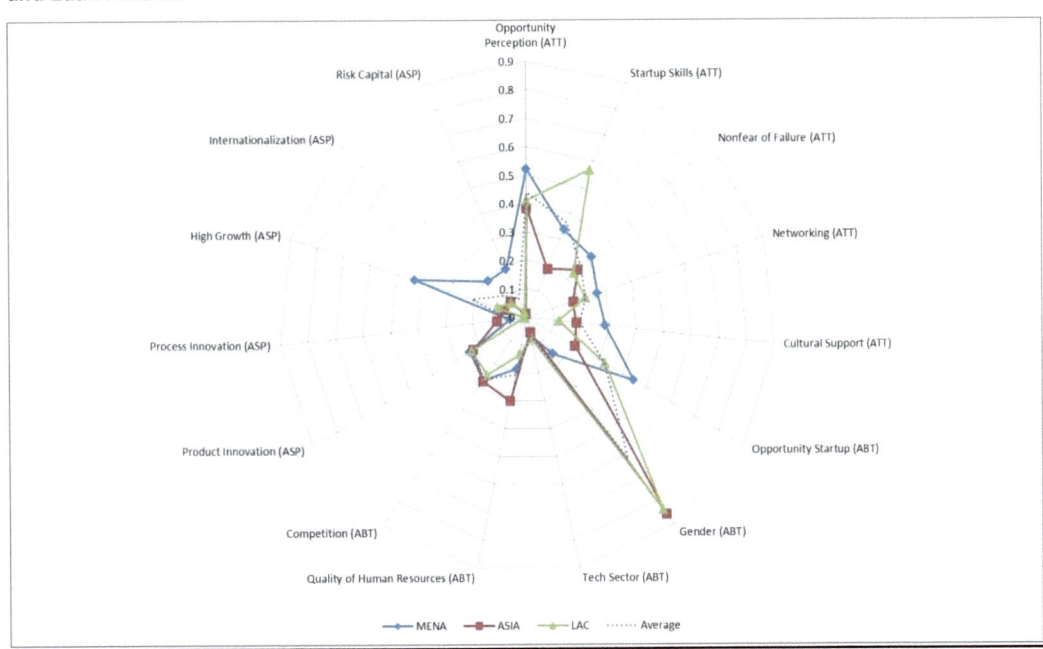

Source: Acs, Szerb, and Autio 2013.
Note: In this spidergram, 0.90 is the maximum value. GEDI pillars are assessed on a scale from 0 to 1.
ASP = aspirations, ABT = ability, ATT= attitudes.
Factor-driven MENA: Algeria, Iran, Morocco, Saudi Arabia, Syria.
Factor-driven Asia: India, Pakistan, Philippines.
Factor-driven LAC: Bolivia, Honduras, Venezuela.

Despite the existence of common trends among factor-driven countries across the three regions, some regional specificities are worth noting. Latin American countries seem to underperform their Asian and MENA counterparts on some indicators, such as process innovation, cultural support, and quality of human resources. Low process and innovation levels stem mainly from the very low levels of public spending on research and development (R&D) as a percentage of GDP. Finances present a problem for all factor-driven economies, but particularly for those in Latin America, as clearly evidenced by low scores on risk capital. On the other hand, Latin America significantly outperforms the other regions in the field of start-up skills. Factor-driven Latin American countries also have average or above-average levels of opportunity start-up, product innovation, networking, and tech sector development.

The potential for high-impact entrepreneurship in Latin America: Case study evidence

To provide additional insight into the drivers of and barriers to the development of high-impact companies in Latin America, the following section presents the main findings of a series of company case studies. These examples of firm creation and development allow us to flesh out the statistical portrait of entrepreneurship presented in the previous section. They also represent a complementary source of qualitative information on how entrepreneurs are incubating and growing high-impact firms in Latin America and the Caribbean.

The case studies presented in the following sections were selected on the basis of four criteria.

- In order to ensure geographical spread, the sample of case studies is drawn from nine different LAC countries, both large and small.

- Case studies were selected on the basis of their impact on markets and communities.

- Case studies include innovations in a variety of sectors and of a variety of types, from high-tech sectors (such as software) to low-tech (such as hair and beauty products), and from product innovations (such as coffee pods) to process innovations.

All of the case studies illustrate to some extent the main challenges, drivers, and opportunities that characterize high-impact entrepreneurship. The case studies are structured around six main themes, based on key determinants of success in high-growth entrepreneurship: (i) product/process innovation, (ii) access to finance, (iii) access to human capital, (iv) access to global markets, (v) cultural support,[6] and (vi) networking. All six themes can be linked to pillars of the GEDI.

Table 1 presents the nine case studies according to country of location, industry, type of innovation, and main elements of interest. Table 2 indicates the relative importance of each theme to the growth and development of the company. The values are estimated by the authors of the case studies. They are important because they give us some indication of how important each theme or pillar is to high-impact entrepreneurship. The estimates are based on the entrepreneurs' views on the importance of each of these themes to starting and growing the company.

Table 1. Characteristics of nine cases of successful entrepreneurship in Latin America

Country	Company	Industry	product innovation	Elements of interest
Argentina	Zauber Labs	Software	High-end software development for a global clientele	Challenges and opportunities to enter global and digital markets The importance of venture capital in high-impact company creation
Bolivia	Origines Bolivia	Manufacturing/ sales	Indigenous art practices for high-end apparel and home goods	Female entrepreneurship Use of local assets to innovate
Brazil	Beleza Natural	Services	Innovative business model for beauty products	Cross-innovation Lipstick economy Addressing the market at the bottom of the pyramid (BOP)
Chile	SmartBoxTV	Information technology	Interactive and integrated applications for digital television, computers, and smart phones	The role of incubators and government programs in firm growth and internationalization
Colombia	Ingerecuperar	Hazardous waste management and recycling	Hazardous waste recovery and recycling solutions	The importance of raising awareness about the success of innovative and niche eco-businesses in nontraditional sectors
Costa Rica	Nature Air	Tourism, green innovation, biofuel production	Green transportation	Use of global markets/standards to distinguish the company from competitors and expand and lead the sustainable travel segment regionally
El Salvador	KAAPS	Manufacturing	Coffee pods	Introducing innovations in mature and well-established sectors/markets

---

[6] Government and culture have been merged. Government can influence all of the pillars.

| Mexico | Aires de Campo | Agribusiness | Organic agriculture and innovative production chain | The creation/transformation of a market segment through technology transfer, product certification, and new product development |
| Peru | Equipar | Manufacturing and service of hyperbaric medical equipment, medical tourism | Cost-effective hyperbaric chambers | Matching global intellectual property to local markets and customers |

Source: Compiled by the authors.

Table 2. The relative Importance of six main themes to case study companies

| | | Degree of importance of theme to company 1 = very important; 2 = important; 3 = not very important | | | | | |
Country	Company	Innovation	Finance	Human Capital	Globalization	Culture	Networking
Argentina	Zauber Software Boutique	1	3	1	1	3	1
Bolivia	Origenes Bolivia	2	2	1	1	3	1
Brazil	Beleza Natural	1	1	1	2	1	1
Chile	SmartBoxTV	1	2	2	1	1	2
Colombia	Ingerecuperar	1	1	3	1	1	3
Costa Rica	Nature Air	1	3	1	1	1	2
El Salvador	KAAPS	1	2	2	2	1	2
Mexico	Aires de Campo	1	2	1	2	2	3
Peru	Equipar Medical SA	1	3	1	1	3	1

Source: Compiled by authors.

The following sections provide an overview of the most salient characteristics of each case study, based on the six main themes presented earlier.

What types of innovations are high-impact entrepreneurs developing in Latin America?

As illustrated by the GEDI results, Latin America has a very weak capacity for process innovations. The case studies analyzed here provide little evidence about why process innovation appears to be more difficult in Latin America than in other parts of the world. They do illustrate, however, that at the micro level, Latin American companies engage in a very wide range of remarkable and unexpected types of innovations.

To begin with, innovators are catering to the needs of a very broad range of markets, from low-income domestic markets to high-purchasing-power global clienteles. This illustrates the high level of adaptability of Latin American entrepreneurs, as well as their capacity to identify opportunity. The sectors in which we find high-impact innovators are also diverse, ranging from information technologies and software to tourism and agriculture.

Zauber Software Boutique and Labs was founded by six engineering students who launched the firm after graduating from Argentina's top technical university. In five years, the company has grown to more than 40 employees in Argentina and Silicon Valley. The firm not only delivers innovative products and services for its clients, but also functions as a laboratory to experiment and grow at the leading edge of its industry, entering markets such as social media and mobile telephony. Zauber's innovative approach to web and software development has led to a growing list of international clients, venture funding, and the spinoff of a separate venture-funded firm based on products developed in-house.

SmartBoxTV is one of Chile's success stories in the information technology (IT) sector. Its applications (apps) for digital TV create new value for telecommunication companies, Over the Top operators, content providers, and consumers. SmartBoxTV apps are innovative products that allow clients to deliver appropriate content at the right time and in synchronicity with existing programming, offering simplicity for the TV viewer and efficiency for the provider. In addition, SmartBoxTV offers more personalized solutions, better communication with clients, and more competitive prices than their direct international competitors, such as ES3.ca and Accedo Broadband. Movistar, one of Chile's most important telecommunication companies, is offering SmartBoxTV apps to its clients.

In comparison to the two previous cases, Beleza Natural, a Brazilian company that makes hair-care products, caters to the needs of lower-income women, a traditionally neglected share of the market. As opposed to Zauber and SmartboxTV, Beleza Natural relies on existing products, technologies, and business models, using them in innovative ways. And, as opposed to companies such as Zauber and SmartboxTV, Beleza Natural's product offering is very weak in terms of technology intensity.

Beleza Natural excels at cross-innovation, taking practices from other industries and adapting them for the beauty salon. In traditional beauty salons, clients typically develop a relationship with an individual hairdresser, rather than the salon. By contrast, Beleza Natural fosters a client's attachment to its brand, not the hairdresser. The company has built its business based on McDonald's fast-food approach by providing top notch, affordable hair care regardless of who is on shift. In addition, like McDonald's, Beleza Natural offers a set menu of 30 haircut styles that have been carefully developed as ideal for kinky hair. As Leila Velez, Beleza Natural's chief executive officer (CEO), comments: "I have no shame in copying" (Ruvolo 2011).

Beleza Natural, which started with a single salon in 1993, currently operates 29 salons and a cosmetics research lab, produces a full line of hair-care products, and employs 1,400 people. In 2012, the company's revenue was more than $30 million.

Beleza Natural is interesting because it is not exclusively a story about female entrepreneurship. Its founders were two women and two men. However, like many successful female-owned businesses, Beleza Natural focused its activities on the demand of an overlooked group, in this case low-income women at the bottom of the pyramid.[7] By offering "affordable luxuries" in the form of hair treatment and the salon experience, Beleza Natural was tapping into the so-called "lipstick economy." However, as is the case for other successful female entrepreneurs, Beleza Natural aspired to provide greater benefits to its clients and employees. The company's business objectives extend to broader social and environmental benefits. These characteristics are found to be more prevalent among female entrepreneurs than male entrepreneurs.

Women who inhabit the market at the bottom of the pyramid form a neglected but substantial segment of the lipstick economy. Businesses that target this segment can improve the welfare of their clients while generating income and profit.

---

[7] The bottom of the pyramid is an economic term referring to the largest but the poorest socioeconomic group in the world, constituting more than 2.5 billion people that live on less than $2.50 a day. C. K. Prahalad and S. L. Hart's book, *Fortune at the Bottom of the Pyramid* (2005) illustrated the idea of targeting clients at the bottom of the pyramid as a viable business strategy.

Examples of successful innovations in the services sector are hard to come by, however. Cases in which innovative service delivery models are developed are often linked to the use or introduction of a new technology. Nature Air of Costa Rica, the world's first carbon-neutral airline, is one such case.

Under the leadership of Alex Khajavi, Nature Air has placed innovation at the center of its brand, strategy, and success. It introduced the production and use of biofuels in Costa Rica, offering more consumer-friendly and environmentally friendly transportation services, while also streamlining its operations, initiating airport recycling programs throughout Costa Rica, and protecting over 300 hectares of forest land in Costa Rica. These innovations have supported the company's expansion from one plane to six, the growth of additional lines of business and international routes, and annual revenues approaching $15 million. Khajavi stated that when he began building Nature Air he had a vision that it could "be a catalyst, [since] we are small enough to be the laboratory of what can be done and how."[8]

The importance of innovation in traditional and well-established sectors such as agriculture and manufacturing should not be underestimated. Despite increasing growth of high-tech sectors in certain clusters of Latin American economies, these countries remain heavily dependent on agricultural production, extractive industries, and industrial manufacturing. Three of the case studies analyzed illustrate the importance of these sectors to Latin American economies. Colombia's Ingerecuperar introduced a novel and environmentally conscious procedure neutralizing hazardous wastes generated by aluminum smelting. KÁAPS has pioneered espresso-making coffee pods in El Salvador. And Aires de Campo in Mexico has pioneered efforts to produce organic products on a large scale.

Ingerecuperar will be discussed further on.

By adding value to coffee, KÁAPS's founders—brothers Eric, Andrés, and Eduardo Roshardt Llort—have carved a niche in a market traditionally dominated by large coffee producers. The coffee pods, previously unknown in El Salvador, are locally produced using high-quality domestic coffee. KÁAPS, from *kaapeh* (coffee in Maya), has evolved on the basis of extensive research. KÁAPS seeks to distinguish itself through a recycling program to minimize its environmental impact. It is also committed to working with local companies and universities, including the Jose Simeon Canas Central American University and Central American Technological Institute (ITCA), to identify not only recycling alternatives but also new packaging materials.[9] KÁAPS is still searching for locally produced packaging materials that meet the company's quality standards. Notwithstanding limited progress on this front, Eric Roshardt remains optimistic that KÁAPS will soon increase the share of locally sourced inputs.

KÁAPS represents one of the few examples of a company that has received early-stage third-party financial support. Its owners conducted a 2010–11 pilot study (Tobar 2012) involving the export of coffee to the United States for packaging in pods, the importation of the finished pods, and their sale in El Salvador. The self-financed study gave the Roshardt brothers a sense of the market size and its potential and proved instrumental to the company's winning the $100,000 PROINNOVA-FUSADES award.[10] These critical funds allowed it to invest in a machine with the capacity to produce up to 60 pods

---

[8] For a video of Khajavi, go to http://www.youtube.com/watch?v=OqDOjj-KToA.

[9] A radio interview with Eric Roshardt aired on May 3, 2012. It is available on "Tenedores y Copas" after minute 49 at http://www.102nueve.com/audio/eln/1336147201.mp3.

[10] FUSADES stands for Fundación Salvadoreña para el Desarrollo Económico y Social (Salvadorian Fundation for Economic and Social Development). In 2008, FUSADES launched the Program for the Promotion of Innovation (PROINNOVA), which relies on a

per minute. FUSADES also paid KÁAPS $15,000 to cover one year of support and assistance. After securing a bank loan with FUSADES's assistance, KÁAPS shifted its focus from financing to strategic market expansion and consolidation.

The experience of Aires de Campo, a pioneer in Mexico's large-scale market for organic products since 2001, illustrates the importance of marketing innovation. An early reliance on direct sales meant very high prices for consumers. At a more fundamental level, it was also very difficult for Aires de Campo to uphold a promise made to its growing network of producers to distribute their certified organic products in the domestic market. The 2005–06 decision to sell a growing variety of certified organic products to large supermarket chains and self-service stores and to expand its home delivery service to Mexico City residents, transformed the company (Clavijo Lopez 2009). Founded to reconnect producers and consumers and so to relaunch Mexico's agricultural economy, Aires de Campo has emerged as an engine of social and environmental transformation in Mexico.[11]

When Aires de Campo began operations in 2001 it had two employees and was funded with money from friends and family. By 2006, the company employed 20 people and also relied on debt to operate. Today, the company has 45 full-time employees and offers more than 500 products from a nationwide network of 150 certified organic producers.

Guadalupe Latapí is the founder of Aires de Campo, one of 20 companies recognized at the 2011 Foro Latinoamericano de Inversión de Impacto (Latin American Forum for Impact Investment) for their environmental and social impact. Since its creation in 2001, the company has contributed to improving the standard of living for low-income people in agricultural communities in Mexico, developed a supply chain for organic products, eliminated pesticides and other agrochemicals from agricultural techniques, and contributed to the development of a growing entrepreneurial culture (Noper Consulting 2012).

Two additional characteristics of the innovations carried out by these companies are worth highlighting. First, there is an increasing incidence of eco-innovation—or innovation that reduces the use of natural resources or decreases the impact of human activity on the environment. Ingerecuperar, Nature Air, KÁAPS, and Aires de Campo all include an environmental component to their innovations. Second, the cases illustrate the importance of female entrepreneurship in Latin America. Nearly half of the companies studied were started by female entrepreneurs engaged in businesses that were socially responsible or environmentally friendly (or both). This supports recent research findings indicating women are more likely to start socially and environmentally conscious businesses than men.[12]

Colombia's Ingerecuperar, co-founded by Carolina Guerra, introduced a novel and environmentally conscious procedure that not only neutralizes hazardous wastes but also recycles it into useful eco-friendly materials. Initially, the company developed a novel method for recycling aluminum dross, a

---

team of national and international advisors to support small and medium-sized enterprises in the food sector. To date, PROINNOVA has provided support to SMEs on business plan development, technology, product improvement, patenting, and linkages with other institutions, including the Fondo de Desarrollo Productivo (FONDEPRO), financial institutions, and universities. As a FONDEPRO Center for Entrepreneurship since 2011, FUSADES also identifies dynamic projects and helps them apply to FONDEPRO for seed capital, according to Camila Contreras, a specialist in business development at FUSADES (contacted by email by the authors).

[11] Phone interview with founder Guadalupe Latapí on May 18, 2012. See also http://www.airesdecampo.com.mx/por_un_mexico_sustentable.asp

[12] A study that analyzed more than 10,000 different entrepreneurs across fifty-two counties found that women were 1.17 times more likely than men to pursue ventures with environmental or social mission statements (Hechevarria et al. 2012).

hazardous byproduct of smelting aluminum for use in automobile manufacturing and food packaging. The company actually purchases the dross since it can make a profit by selling the recycled product, a form of cement that is used to manufacture building blocks, benches, and fence posts. Recently, Ingerecuperar has expanded its recycling operations to include other categories of hazardous waste, including incinerator ash, pipeline powder, and lead-based wastes from battery production. Ingerecuperar is the first and only company in Colombia to obtain an environmental license for aluminum dross recycling.

Ingerecuperar's operates in a male-dominated sector that is characterized by informality. Initially, Carolina Guerra was viewed as "female," implying weakness and vulnerability. These attitudes changed as Ingerecuperar became more visible and profitable. The first recognition of Guerra's success came from an international organization (she received Cartier's Women's Initiative Award), which ultimately led to greater recognition, credibility, and support in Colombia. Her case illustrates the pivotal role international organizations can play in supporting and fostering female entrepreneurship in Latin America.

How are high-impact companies financed at the early stages of development?

Financing is key to successful innovation and entrepreneurship. The GEDI results for Latin America show the extent to which it remains a critical barrier to the development of high-impact companies and the innovations that support them in Latin America. While self-financing for innovative start-ups is not uncommon, the large number of companies in this report that were created with the entrepreneurs' own resources is noteworthy. Among these cases we find a wide range of entrepreneurial experience, from first-time bootstrapping to serial entrepreneurship. Furthermore, some businesses were able to obtain financing through awards, whereas, for others, increased visibility from market expansion facilitated bank loans and investor funding.

Table 3 provides an overview of the funding sources leading to the launch of seven of the companies analyzed.

Table 3. Funding sources for the creation of seven firms profiled in this study

Company	Start-up funding
Zauber Software Lab and Boutique	Three of the founders worked full time out of a basement to start the firm, while the other three kept traditional jobs to provide cash flow for initial operations. Within four months the firm had enough cash flow from operations to hire its first two employees. Zauber continued to self-finance and grow organically until its daily deal e-commerce website, Cupoint, raised $700,000 in late 2011. Shortly thereafter, in April 2012, Zauber Lab received a $1 million equity investment.,The company is now poised to grow beyond its forty-five employees.
Beleza Natural	The company's start-up capital came from the sale of a co-founder's Volkswagen Beetle. Beleza Natural has been continuously self-financed throughout its sustained high growth. Although the four founders recognized their market potential, others were skeptical. In fact, Beleza Natural was initially unable even to open a bank account.
SmartboxTV	SmartboxTV has won several awards from government-sponsored programs and from Movistar Innova, the first private incubator and business accelerator in Chile, for its innovativeness and growth potential. Although the financial prizes associated with these awards have amounted to more than $120,000, the three founders have relied primarily on personal funds and debt to fund the operation.
Ingerercuperar	The three founders contributed start-up capital totaling $50,000, which covered the purchase of necessary machinery and other costs associated with recycling aluminum dross.
KÁAPS	The company represents one of the few examples that has received early-stage third-party financial support. After conducting a self-financed study, the company received $100,000 from the PROINNOVA-FUSADES award. After securing a bank loan with FUSADES's assistance, KÁAPS shifted its focus from financing to strategic market expansion and consolidation.
Aires de Campo	The company was launched with money from the founders' friends and family. Ten years after its launch, 50 percent of the company was sold to a large market leader.
Equipar	Equipar Medical's Gary Urteaga, a serial entrepreneur, leveraged one of his ventures to support the growth of another.

How does the availability of qualified human capital contribute to high-impact entrepreneurship?

As reflected in our case studies, the concept of human capital covers a range of issues. Some entrepreneurs consider their own educational backgrounds to be an important factor in their success, while others credit their involvement in training and educating employees and producers. In one case, a major factor in the development of the company was the strategic decision to locate operations in an area known for its availability of industry-specific, skilled human capital.

Human capital is at the heart of the success of Zauber Software Boutique and Lab, as its six founders were classmates and graduates of Argentina's leading technical college, Instituto Tecnológico de Buenos Aires (ITBA). In launching Zauber, they agreed that the global market for high-end software and web development was within their reach—access to human capital would enable success in those growing markets. Zauber's policy of participating in open source development and hosting hackathons[13] highlights its commitment to human capital development. Over five years, the company has grown to 45 people, raised $1 million in venture financing, spun out a venture-funded, 10-person web commerce firm, and established offices in Buenos Aires and Silicon Valley, supporting the founders' vision of hiring the brightest minds to build software and web products and services.

---

[13] According to Wikipedia, "a hackathon (also known as a hack day, hackfest, or codefest) is an event in which computer programmers and others involved in software development, including graphic designers, interface designers, and project managers, collaborate intensively on software projects."

Claudia Maria Mendez, the founder of Origenes Bolivia, studied in the United States, obtaining a master's degree in economics from the University of Texas. The vast majority of the indigenous artisans who produce the upscale apparel and textiles sold by Origenes Bolivia, however, are poorly educated women who work from home. Given the lack of paid day care in Bolivia, working from home provides many advantages for mothers, especially single mothers, allowing them to care for their children while earning an income. Most of these artisans never legalize their businesses and so are unable to register for medical or social benefits. Origenes Bolivia explicitly aims to empower them. Maria Claudia Mendez provides training in areas such as product quality, business formalization, and the advantages of paying into the system for medical insurance and social security benefits.

None of Beleza Natural's founders had college degrees or formal business education. Leila Velez, Beleza Natural's CEO, who started working at McDonald's when she was 14 years old, jokes that she received a "McDonald's MBA." Ten years after co-founding the company, however, she earned a bachelor's degree in business administration and went on to receive an executive MBA. Recognizing the importance of education, Beleza Natural offers extensive training and health benefits to employees (even during the training period) and promotes further professional development by offering them tuition discounts of 30 to 50 percent at several local universities.

At Aires de Campo, a key driver of success has been the strong emphasis on training employees and producers. Employees are offered detailed training in organic produce, as well as a theoretical and practical introduction to all other areas of the company. The company also supports producers interested in pursuing organic certification or learning more about new product development, product packaging, or environmentally friendly production processes. Aires de Campo has also reached out to clients and consumers, offering occasional talks about its products, meeting with clients to evaluate customer satisfaction, and providing recipes on its website, as well as insights into environmental impacts and the growth of the organic market.

What role do globalization and international networks play in the development of high-impact companies?

The internationalization pillar of the GEDI for efficiency-driven economies shows significant disparities among Europe, Asia, and Latin America. European entrepreneurs seem far more exposed to the international arena and develop stronger international partnerships than their Asian or Latin American counterparts. Looking at individual countries, we see that internationalization is the weakest pillar in the large Latin American economies. The ability to expand internationally is key to the success of most high-impact entrepreneurs. A number of related issues came up in our case studies as well. For some companies, market openness in the form of free-trade agreements was important for facilitating exports. For others, capitalizing on past international experiences was a way to leverage international deals and further cultivate global ties and linkages. Setting up operations in a key overseas market was another strategy for expanding international access.

The case studies also illustrate the pivotal role international awards played in increasing the credibility and visibility of this group of successful entrepreneurs. In addition to the financial support obtained through the awards, companies benefited from access to new partners, mentors, knowledge, and support networks. Examples of these awards follow.

- Origenes Bolivia (Bolivia), Maria Claudia Mendez, owner
  - The *Fortune*/U.S. Department of State/Vital Voices mentoring program, 2005

- Beleza Natural (Brazil), Leila Velez, CEO
  - Ernst and Young's Entrepreneur of the Year, 2006
  - High-Impact Female Entrepreneur of the Year award from Veuve Clicquot, 2011[14]
- Ingerecuperar (Colombia), Carolina Guerra, co-founder
  - Cartier's Women's Initiative Award, 2011[15]
- Equipar Medical (Peru), Gary Urteaga, CEO
  - MYPE President's Prize for top entrepreneur from the Peruvian government, 2010
- Nature Air (Costa Rica), Alex Khajavi, CEO
  - Sustainable Innovators Award from the Rain Forest Alliance, 2009
  - Geotourism Challenge from the National Geographic Society, 2009
  - Global Vision Award from *Travel and Leisure* magazine, 2011

As illustrated by the examples below, the exposure to international networks, markets, and knowledge provided by such awards proved a key driver of growth in several cases.

Maria Claudia Mendez identified exporting as Origenes Bolivia's main strategy. She initially targeted the U.S. market, attending the largest U.S. trade show (the annual Magic trade show in Las Vegas) in search of buyers. There she was able to build a network of 50 U.S.-based boutiques that would purchase her merchandise. At the same time, she expanded exports to Canada, Europe, Japan, Korea, and Mexico. Unfortunately, Origenes Bolivia's further expansion in the U.S. market was curtailed in 2011 when the Bolivian government rejected an extension of its free-trade agreement with the United States. Paying duties for exports to the United States was too costly, and Origenes Bolivia had to reorient its business strategy to focus on expanding exports to Europe, as well as on domestic sales through its two boutique shops.

Ingerecuperar is orienting its export strategy based on Colombia's free-trade agreements with the United States and South Korea. The company believes both markets will provide export opportunities for its aluminum dross recycled building materials, which are suitable for LEED-certified[16] prefabricated construction projects.

The design and content of Zauber Software Boutique and Lab's website clearly show that the firm is global in its approach, reach, and mindset. From its list of international clients, such as Coca-Cola and Al Jazeera, to its offices in Buenos Aires and Silicon Valley, the company's evolution highlights the global nature of technology development and markets. With its lean and agile development strategies, Zauber

---

[14] Veuve Cliquot, a premium champagne house, created its annual Business Women Awards in 1972. The High Impact Female of the Year award is a more recent addition, created in partnership with Endeavor and the Endeavor Entrepreneur Summit.

[15] The Cartier Women's Initiative Awards are an international business plan competition created in 2006 by Cartier, the Women's Forum, McKinsey & Company, and INSEAD business school in France. The awards aim to encourage the most vulnerable category of entrepreneurs—women—in their most vulnerable phase of starting up. One winner from each of the six regions is selected, based on the quality of the plan presented and the ability of the presenter to demonstrate exceptional creativity, financial sustainability, and social impact. Each of the six winners receives a Cartier Women's Initiative Award trophy, one year of personalized coaching, and $20,000 in funding. For further information, see http://www.cartierwomensinitiative.com.

[16] Leadership in Energy and Environmental Design (LEED) is an internationally recognized green building certification system.

has firmly established itself in emerging technology markets, proving that entrepreneurs with top technical skills can emerge anywhere and have a global impact. Zauber's products, services, clients, investors, and partners are evidence that global growth industries such as software and web development are quick to recognize and integrate talented firms, regardless of where they are founded.

Gary Urteaga, founder of Equipar Medical, has repeatedly made use of global networks and partners to grow his medical device firm and other new ventures that rely on technological innovations. He drew not only on his family's background in medical equipment, but also his graduate school experience in Japan and the United States. During his time in Japan, Urteaga won a prize for his work on drug importation with a Swedish biotech firm. He also gained experience in technology markets while working for an internet firm in Florida and with the United Nations as a global investment analyst. In 2007, while leading Equipar, Urteaga leveraged his background to secure a deal with a U.S. firm that would bring the production of hyperbaric chambers to Peru. Equipar Medical's growth reflects the global background and experiences of the founder and his partners.

SmartboxTV's global outlook is a necessity in Internet protocol television, known as IPTV. The eight interactive applications on its website are for Spanish speakers around the world. These include TwitVid, which combines a Twitter feed with TV content, allowing users to comment on what they are watching; facetv, "[the easiest] way to recommend your favorite TV show [and] check the latest photos, top feeds, and [more], using [your] remote control"; PostTV, "an application that allows users to leave messages on the TV screen from virtually any device"; and InteractiveSport, an online application that reports the results of sports competitions worldwide and allows users to review information about upcoming games, vote for the best player on the field, or even follow the comments by the major social networks.[17] The firm's founders clearly recognize the company's potential in a fast-growing global market. Indeed, they have made a point of developing its applications for all leading interactive platforms, establishing global partnerships with Microsoft Mediaroom, LG, Alcatel-Lucent, Sagemcom, and others. In 2011, Chile's Corporación de Fomento de la Producción (Corfo) and the prestigious Silicon Valley incubator, Plug and Play Tech Center, awarded SmartboxTV $20,000 and the opportunity to spend three months in Silicon Valley working on internationalization.[18]

How do government action and culture influence high-impact entrepreneurship?

GEDI scores for cultural support are remarkably consistent for all efficiency-driven economies. Looking at the large Latin American economies, we see that Brazil actually scores well above Mexico and Argentina and just below Chile. The cases have varied greatly, however, with regard to government and culture-related issues. In some cases, the entrepreneurs were able to capitalize on proactive government policies supporting innovation in key areas. In others, they described bureaucratic impediments and interference from regional and national officials that hindered business operations.

Costa Rica's policies and signals on sustainability were known to Alex Khajavi and his Nature Air Group when they chose the country as the site for the world's first carbon-neutral airline. Since the

---

[17] See http://www.smartboxtv.com.

[18] "Emprendedores de SmartboxTV abrirán oficina en Silicon Valley gracias a Global Connection," May 18, 2011, http://www.movistarinnova.cl/blog/noticias/noticias/emprendedores-chilenos-viajaran-a-silicon-valley-para-internacionalizar-sus-negocios, accessed May 27, 2012. See also "Emprendedores chilenos viajarán a Silicon Valley para internacionalizar sus negocios," *ikwest play & explore*, May 18, 2011, http://outdoors.ikwest.com/index.php?option=com_content&view=article&id=43%3Asv&catid=2%3Anoticias&Itemid=24&lang =es, accessed May 15, 2012.

establishment of its acclaimed national park system in 1969, Costa Rica has enacted clear policies protecting the environment. The Costa Rican Tourism Board (ICT) is charged with promoting sustainable tourism, encouraging "wholesome tourism development, with the purpose of improving Costa Ricans' quality of life by maintaining a balance between economic and social boundaries, environmental protection, culture, and facilities."[19] In 1997, ICT began offering a voluntary Certification for Sustainable Tourism Program for providers of lodging, which was expanded considerably to include tour operators, car rental firms, and others.[20] The program measures and certifies the sustainability of a firm's business models. While Nature Air's work—increasing efficiency to lower fuel consumption, producing and using biofuels, and protecting 3,000 hectares of Costa Rican forest—does not fit within the sustainable tourism certification program, the experience highlights the importance of building high-growth firms that support national and international objectives such as sustainable tourism.

SmartboxTV has been active in StartUp Chile, a government program that, according to Rafael López, has helped foster an entrepreneurial climate by offering entrepreneurs who want to start their businesses in Chile one-year working visas, $40,000 (equity free), and access to one of the biggest entrepreneurial communities in Latin America. After learning about Chile's awards programs through StartUp Chile, SmartboxTV has won several awards from government-sponsored programs promoting entrepreneurship, innovation, and internationalization. It has also twice received support from Movistar Innova, the first private incubator and business accelerator in Chile.[21] An award from Chile's Corporación de Fomento de la Producción (Corfo), a government entity that promotes entrepreneurship and innovation in Chile, gave SmartboxTV access to $100,000 in 2010,[22] and in 2011 (as described in the previous section), the company received $20,000 as part of the Global Connection program supported by Corfo and Plug and Play Tech Center. Recently, SmartboxTV was awarded $10,000 from ProChile. These awards have benefited SmartboxTV tremendously. Not only do they offer recognition for the quality and potential of the company's apps, they also provide access to important business networks, funds, and know-how.

According to Eric Roshardt, co-founder of KÁAPS, El Salvador is a country of enormous opportunity where "there is support for people with good ideas and willingness to work hard" (Quintanilla 2012). A major breakthrough for KÁAPS was winning the 2012 PROINNOVA—FUSADES award,[23] which provided funds from the Fondo de Desarrollo Productivo (FONDEPRO) of the Ministry of Economy to buy the coffee pod–producing machine that enabled local production. But getting things done in the country still takes a tremendous amount of effort. Patience is necessary when applying for permits, especially when the company is a pioneer in a new market. Still, KÁAPS expects to rely on PROESA and FONDEPRO for help in meeting the challenges ahead (for example, in seeking to import coffee temporarily from other countries to create the KÁAPS pods).

---

[19] http://www.visitcostarica.com/ict/paginas/TourismBoard.asp.

[20] Visit the ICT CST site for more details on the program's history and functioning, as well as participants: www.turismo-sostenible.co.cr/.

[21] "La primera incubadora privada de Chile y Latinoamérica," *Ediciones Especiales Online*, June 17, 2011, http://www.edicionesespeciales.elmercurio.com/destacadas/detalle/index.asp?idnoticia=20110617743142&idcuerpo=969, accessed May 15, 2012.

[22] InnovaChile, a unit of Corfo, offers an array of support services for innovative and entrepreneurial companies: http://www.corfo.cl/.

[23] "FUSADES y FONDEPRO firman convenio de emprendimiento, *El Mundo*, February 24, 2012, http://elmundo.com.sv/fusades-y-fondepro-firman-convenio-de-emprendimiento, accessed May 30, 2012.

Leila Velez, Beleza Natural's CEO, feels Brazil offers tremendous potential, especially given the size of its market and its booming economy. But businesses face a number of impediments there. The bureaucracy can be overwhelming. Since local officials lacked confidence in the firm's strategy of targeting low-income clients, Beleza Natural had to wait an entire year before getting the green light to open its cosmetics factory. When Beleza Natural needed assistance to expand internationally, the company approached the U.S. nonprofit Endeavor, essentially going abroad for business support.

What role do personal and professional networks play in supporting high-impact entrepreneurial activity?

The GEDI results under the networking pillar are also very consistent for efficiency-driven economies across Europe, Asia, and Latin America. Networking appears key to the success of the companies in our case studies. There are two types of networks: business and personal. Especially in the start-up phase, some entrepreneurs considered personal international networks a crucial source of inspiration, boosting their morale to forge ahead and develop their businesses. Business-related networks were also important, especially as a means to overcome limited resources. Some also described the cultivation of client networks as a useful strategy to spur growth, develop new products and services, and gain trust and loyalty.

In 2005, two years after starting Origenes Bolivia, Maria Claudia Mendez was feeling isolated and ready to close her business. Most important, she had no peers who shared similar experiences and could offer her support. Vital Voices,[24] a nonprofit organization that focuses on promoting women's economic empowerment, invited her to take part in a mentoring program supported by Fortune and the U.S. Department of State,[25] which included a week of leadership training in Washington, DC, and three weeks with a mentor. Sixteen other women from thirteen different countries also participated. The program sensitized Mendez to the importance of working with other women to overcome common barriers, and she took encouragement from their experiences, which reminded her that every entrepreneur faces a unique set of difficulties. Mendez returned to Bolivia full of inspiration to grow Origenes Bolivia.

Given their resource constraints, successful entrepreneurs must rely on networking to benefit from the strengths and assets of others in building their firms. Serial entrepreneur Gary Urteaga has repeatedly used global networking to gain technical advantages for his Peru-based firms, Equipar Medical and Papaya.pe. Urteaga's work and educational experiences abroad proved an asset when he partnered with U.S. firms to bring hyperbaric chamber production to Peru. Additionally, Equipar leveraged international networks to grow his online video firm Papaya.pe. Urteaga and his partner used the firm's early success to participate in Intel's Global Challenge Program in Berkeley, California, in 2011. The company was also chosen from among more than 1,200 firms to participate in Wayra, a technology-accelerated program

---

[24] Vital Voices is a U.S.-based nongovernmental organization established in 1997 that focuses its activities for women in three main areas: human rights, public and political leadership, and economic empowerment. It boasts an international staff and a team of more than 1,000 partners, pro bono experts, and leaders from government, business, and the nonprofit sector who have trained and mentored more than 12,000 emerging women leaders from at least 144 countries in Africa, Asia, Eurasia, Latin America and the Caribbean, and the Middle East. These women have returned home to train and mentor more than 500,000 additional women and girls in their communities (http://www.vitalvoices.com).

[25] The International Women Leaders Mentoring Partnership brings young businesswomen from around the world to intern with some of the world's most powerful women. CEO Ann Moore and the U.S. State Department, working with America's embassies around the world, nominate the interns. Vital Voices, an international nonprofit chaired by Melanie Verveer (formerly Hilary Clinton's chief of staff when she was first lady) helps administer the program. In 2006, seventeen women from fourteen countries participated in Vital Voices.

funded and supported by Telefonica of Spain. Wayra is a digital initiative that aims to promote innovation and identify talent in Latin America and Europe in the field of information and communication technologies. According to its website, Wayra's "global project acceleration model helps entrepreneurs develop, providing them with technological tools, qualified mentors, a cutting-edge work space, and the financing required to accelerate their growth."[26] Urteaga and his partners have used global networks to strengthen their firms and bring more high-growth, high-impact firms to Peru.

In terms of internationalization prospects, SmartboxTV benefited greatly from its early relationship with Movistar, as the multinational Telefónica is called in Chile. In 2012, SmartboxTV founders toured Europe, offering their interactive apps to contacts made through Movistar/Telefónica's international network. Under Aceleración, Movistar Innova's business acceleration program, Movistar retains the option to buy a certain percentage of the company in return for the access and business advice it has provided. SmartboxTV has also developed important relationships with both new and experienced entrepreneurs. After winning the Global Connection award, the company's founders spent three months in Silicon Valley working on a business plan for international expansion. As Rafael López shares in his blog, the experience allowed them to meet potential clients, partners, investors, and even their direct competitors.[27]

For KÁAPS to sell coffee pods in other Central American countries, it must consider the strong, persistent feelings among consumers there regarding the consumption of imported coffee, even from El Salvador, when an alternative of equal quality can be found domestically. Accordingly, KÁAPS is conducting joint research in Central America with contacts whom the Roshardt brothers know or have made at fairs. In fact, contacts have always been essential to the company's development. As a small player, KÁAPS cultivated each of its large clients, hotels, and restaurants individually, afraid of tipping off powerful coffee producers to the opportunity. As their brand recognition continues to grow, it is not uncommon to hear consumers asked if they "want a KÁAPS" instead of "a coffee." KÁAPS launched a marketing campaign in the second half of 2012.

Beleza Natural champions the maintenance of friendly client relations in three specific ways. First, it hires employees directly from its customer base (70 percent of its 1,400 employees were clients). Second, its customers provide the inspiration and ideas for product development—all of Beleza Natural's products have been co-created with customer input. Third, Beleza Natural continues to make use of social media such as Orkut, Facebook, Twitter, and a user-friendly company website and blog (Barki 2011).

Conclusion: Policy themes

This discussion was not intended to provide specific policy recommendations to drive high-impact entrepreneurship. Instead, our intention was to identify some of the key barriers to and drivers of the development of high-impact companies in Latin America. We did this by analyzing results drawn from the GEDI, as well as empirical evidence from real cases. These lessons are meant to support the design and implementation of sound policies and programs aimed at driving growth through high-impact companies.

---

[26] http://www.wayra.org/es/que-te-ofrecemos.

[27] http://www.smartboxtv.com/2012/01/el-verdadero-valle-de-silicio/.

Despite very distinct country specificities across Latin American economies, entrepreneurship systems in this region apparently face a common set of strengths and weaknesses that affect the birth and growth of high-impact companies.

First and foremost, lack of access to risk capital is a critical impediment to high-impact entrepreneurship in the region. The large majority of cases presented here were self-financed in their early stages and able to thrive in environments where outside financing was practically nonexistent. Many entrepreneurs launched their start-up operations on shoestring budgets. Notably, in several cases, the entrepreneurs secured funds from international awards or by utilizing their international networks and contacts. As all entrepreneurs are not so lucky, however, improving access to risk capital from both informal investors and venture capitalists should be considered an important first step in supporting high-impact companies.

International awards, training programs, and mentorship at critical junctures of business development are an underlying theme in many of the case studies. International awards, in particular, gave many of these entrepreneurs local prestige that translated into credibility and visibility, attracting new clients and investors. Such benefits should not be underestimated. More national or regional awards could multiply this effect for Latin American entrepreneurs. Also, training and mentoring programs provide benefits beyond new skills.

Access to education is another thread that runs through most of these cases. Many of these entrepreneurs earned advanced degrees abroad, most often in the United States. Education has been found to be an important attribute of opportunity-motivated, successful entrepreneurs. On a related note, several of the entrepreneurs discussed here were committed to training their employees and producers, which seemed to fill gaps in the educational opportunities in their respective countries. Successful high-impact entrepreneurs need the skills to launch and run their businesses, but they also need a well-trained pool of prospective employees to succeed.

Internationalization and access to export markets worldwide form another important driver for high-impact company growth. In a number of the cases presented, the entrepreneurs were successful because they were able to orient their growing operations toward overseas clients. This macro-dimension of high-impact entrepreneurship may often go overlooked, but it is key to fostering business growth. Access to international markets is cultivated through open market policies that embrace free-trade agreements and other international forums that stimulate export development.

High-impact entrepreneurs are, almost by definition, innovative, often developing unexpected and unique products or services. As several of these cases indicate, in some Latin American countries, innovative entrepreneurs must not only sell their products or services to potential customers; they must also sell the viability of their business concepts to local regulatory officials to get certification and documents. Instead of letting the market decide if a product or service will be viable, officials in the region often interfere with the process of entering the market.

Finally, policy makers are sometimes faced with the difficult task of selecting the sectors in which they would like to see high-impact companies emerge. While high-technology sectors such as information and communication technology seem to be flourishing in Latin America, the importance of more traditional and mature sectors, such as agriculture and manufacturing, should not be neglected. Promoting the emergence of innovation there not only provides a means to increase productivity and competitiveness in sectors employing large sections of the population; it also helps diversify economic activity and open up new markets. Supporting eco-innovation, for instance, could represent a way of cutting across a number of sectors while linking innovation to the sustainability agenda.

Latin America and the Caribbean is not yet a hotbed of high-impact entrepreneurship. Despite the existence of multiple examples of very successful high-impact companies in a wide variety of sectors, the region faces strong structural problems that limit their more widespread development. In particular, the region particularly lacks entrepreneurial aspiration, as illustrated by its low levels of process innovations, high growth aspiration, and risk capital.

Based on this analysis, the Latin American region could round out its development strategy and reinforce its entrepreneurial capacity with targeted interventions to increase credit and the inflow of venture capital, and by more effectively promoting R&D and technology transfer SMEs (Acs and Szerb 2012).

References

Acs, Z. J., B. Carlsson, and C. and Karlsson. 1999. *Entrepreneurship, Small and Medium-Sized Enterprises and the Macroeconomy*. Cambridge University Press.

Acs, Z. J., E. Autio, and L. Szerb. 2014. National Systems of Entrepreneurship: Measurement Issues and Policy Implications, *Research Policy* 43, 476-494.

Acs, Z. J., and L. Szerb. 2012. "The 2012 Global Entrepreneurship and Development Index (GEDI): Perspectives from the Americas." Heritage Foundation, Washington, DC, and George Mason University, Fairfax, VA. http://eagle.gmu.edu/newsroom/files/GEDI.pdf.

Acs, Z. J., L. Szerb, and E. Autio. 2013. *The Global Entrepreneurship and Development Index 2013.* Edward Elgar.

Acs, Z. J., P. Braunerhjelm, D. B. Audretsch, and B. Carlsson. 2009. A Knowledge Spillover Theory of Entrepreneurship. *Small Business Economics*, 32(1): 15–30.

Ahmad, N., and A. Hoffmann. 2008. A Framework for Addressing and Measuring Entrepreneurship. SSRN eLibrary.

Alvarez, S. A., and J. Barney. 2007. Discovery and Creation: Alternative Theories of Entrepreneurial Action. *Strategic Entrepreneurship Journal* 1(1–2): 33–48.

Audretsch, D. B. 2007. *The Entrepreneurial Society.* New York: Oxford University Press.

———. 2009. Emergence of the Entrepreneurial Society. *Economic and Social Review* 40(3): 255–68.

Audretsch, D. B., and M. Keilbach. 2008. Resolving the Knowledge Paradox: Knowledge-Spillover Entrepreneurship and Economic Growth. *Research Policy* 37(10): 1697–1705.

Audretsch, D. B., and A. R. Thurik. 2001. What Is New about the New Economy: Sources of Growth in the Managed and Entrepreneurial Economies. *Industrial and Corporate Change* 10: 267–315.

Autio, E. 2007. GEM 2007 Report on High-Growth Entrepreneurship. GEM Global Reports. London: GERA.

Autio, E., M. Cleevely, M. Hart, J. Levie, Z. Acs, and L. Szerb. 2012. Entrepreneurial Profile of the UK in the Light of the Global Entrepreneurship and Development Index. Innovation and Entrepreneurship Group Working Papers 35. London: Imperial College Business School.

Autio, E., M. Kronlund, and A. Kovalainen. 2007. High-Growth SME Support Initiatives in Nine Countries: Analysis, Categorization, and Recommendations. Industries Department, Ministry of Trade and Industry, Helsinki.

Birch, D. 1979. The Job Generation Process. Unpublished MS Thesis, Massachusetts Institute of Technology, Cambridge, MA.

Birch, D., A. Haggerty, and W. Parsons. 1997. *Who's Creating Jobs?* Cambridge, MA: Cognetics.

Bosma, N., Z. Acs, E. Autio, A. Coduras, and J. Levie. 2009. Global Entrepreneurship Monitor 2008. Executive Report 65. London: GERA.

Coduras, A., and E. Autio. 2012. Tracking National Entrepreneurial Framework Conditions: A Preliminary Review of the Global Entrepreneurship Monitor Expert's Survey and Its Comparison with the World Economic Forum's Executive Opinion Survey. GEM Research Workshop. San Sebastian, Spain.

Djankov, S., R. La Porta, F. Lopez-de-Silanes, and A. Shleifer. 2002. The Regulation of Entry. *Quarterly Journal of Economics*, 117(1): 453–517.

Dreher, Axel. 2006. "Does Globalization Affect Growth? Evidence from a New Index of Globalization." *Applied Economics* 38(10): 1091–1110.

Freeman, C. 1988. Japan: A New National System of innovçation? In G. Dosi, C. Freeman, R. Nelson, G. Silverberg, and L. L. G. Soete (eds.), *Technical Change and Economic Theory* (312–29). London: Pinter.

Freytag, A., and A. R. Thurik. 2007. Entrepreneurship and Its Determinants in a Cross-Country Setting. *Journal of Evolutionary Economics* 17(2): 117–31.

Gallup Organization. 2009. Entrepreneurship in the EU and Beyond. *Flash Eurobarometer* 283. Brussels: European Commission.

Grilo, I., and A. R. Thurik. 2005. Latent and Actual Entrepreneurship in Europe. *International Entrepreneurship and Management Journal* 1(4): 441–59.

Groh, A., H. Liechtenstein, and K. Lieser. 2012. The Global Venture Capital and Private Equity Country Attractiveness Index 2012 Annual Report. http://blog.iese.edu/vcpeindex/about/.

Henrekson, M., and M. Stenkula. 2009. Entrepreneurship and Public Policy. Working Paper Series 804, Research Institute of Industrial Economics, Stockholm.

Hoffmann, A., M. Larsen, and A. S. Oxholm. 2006. Quality Assessment of Entrepreneurship Indicators. In I. C. f. D. B. o. Entrepreneurship (ed.) 187. Copenhagen: FORA.

Hofstede, G. 2001. *Culture's Consequences: Comparing Values, Behaviors, Institutions and Organizations Across Nations* (2nd ed.). Thousand Oaks, CA: Sage.

ISSP (International Social Survey Programme). 1997. Work Orientations Package II. In L. Gemeinschaft (ed.). Berlin: Leibniz Gemeinschaft.

Javidan, M., R. J. House, P. W. Dorfman, P. J. Hanges, and M. S. Luque. 2006. Conceptualizing and Measuring Cultures and Their Consequences: A Comparative Review of GLOBE's and Hofstede's Approaches. *Journal of International Business Studies* 37(6): 897–914.

Kirzner, I. 1997. Entrepreneurial Discovery and the Competitive Market Process: An Austrian Approach. *Journal of Economic Literature* 35: 60–85.

Kirzner, L. 1973. *Competition and Entrepreneurship*. Chicago: University of Chicago Press.

Leibenstein, H. 1978. *General X-Efficiency Theory and Economic Development*. New York: Oxford University Press.

Levie, J., and M. Hart. 2012. The Global Entrepreneurship Monitor United Kingdom 2011 Monitoring Report 37. Birmingham: Aston Business School and the Hunter Centre for Entrepreneurship, University of Strathclyde.

Lunati, M., J. Meyer zu Schlochtern, and G. Sargsayan. 2010. Measuring Entrepreneurship. In OECD (Ed.), Vol. 15: 12. Paris: OECD.

Lundvall, B.-Å. (Ed.). 1992. *National Systems of Innovations*. London: Pinter.

Nelson, R. R. (ed.). 1993. *National Innovation Systems: A Comparative Analysis*. New York: Oxford University Press.

OECD (Organisation for Economic Co-operaiton and Development). 2010. "High-Growth Enterprises: What Governments Can Do to Make a Difference." OECD Studies on SMEs and Entrepreneurship, Paris.

OECD-Eurostat. 2007. Eurostat-OECD Manual on Business Demography Statistics. Paris.

Radosevic, S. 2007. National Systems of Innovation and Entrepreneurship: In Search of a Missing Link. Economics Working Papers 51. London: University College.

Reynolds, P. D. 2007. *Entrepreneurship in the United States: The Future Is Now*. International Studies in Entrepreneurship 15. Springer.

Reynolds, P. D., N. Bosma, and E. Autio. 2005. Global Entrepreneurship Monitor: Data Collection Design and Implementation, 1998–2003. *Small Business Economics* 24(3): 205–31.

Robinson, W. S. 1950. Ecological Correlation and the Behavior of Individuals. *American Sociological Review* 15(July): 351–57.

Schmid, A. 2004. *Conflict and Cooperation. Institutional and Behavioural Economics*. London: Blackwell.

Schoar, A. 2009. *The Divide between Subsistence and Transformational Entrepreneurship.* NBER Innovation Policy and the Economy. Available at: http://www.mit.edu/~aschoar/SubsistenceVsTransformationalEntrepreneurs.pdf

Schramm, C. J. 2008. Economic Fluidity: A Crucial Dimension of Economic Freedom. In *2008 Index of Economic Freedom* (chapter 1). Washington, DC: Heritage Foundation.

Seligson, M. A. 2002. The Renaissance of Political Culture or the Renaissance of the Ecological Fallacy. *Comparative Politics* 34(April): 273–92.

Shane, S., and S. Venkataraman. 2000. The Promise of Entrepreneurship as a Field of Research. *Academy of Management Review* 25(1): 217–26.

Uhlaner, L., and R. Thurik. 2007. "Post-Materialism: A Cultural Factor Influencing Total Entrepreneurial Activity Across Nations. *Journal of Evolutionary Economics* 17(2): 161–85.

World Bank. 2011. New Business Registration Database 2011. Washington, DC.

Appendix 1. The individual variables used in the GEDI

Individual variable	Description
Opportunity recognition	The percentage of the population aged 18–64 years believing that there will be good opportunities to start a business in their area over the next six months.
Skill perception	The percentage of the population aged 18–64 years claiming to possess the required knowledge and skills to start a business.
Risk acceptance	The percentage of the population aged 18–64 years stating that fear of failure would *not* prevent them from starting a business.
Acquaintance with entrepreneurs	The percentage of the population aged 18–64 years having a personal acquaintance who started a business in the past two years.
Career	The percentage of the population aged 18–64 years stating that people in their country believe starting a business to be a good career choice.
Status	The percentage of the population aged 18–64 years stating that people in their country accord high status to successful entrepreneurs.
Career status	The status and respect accorded entrepreneurs, calculated as the average of the previous two variables.
Opportunity motivation	The percentage of TEA businesses initiated because the entrepreneur saw an opportunity for a start-up.
TEA female	Ratio between female TEA and male TEA (1:1 ratio is considered the best value, and deviations in either direction are considered suboptimal).
Technology level	Percentage of TEA businesses that are active in technology sectors (high-tech or mid-range).
Educational level	Percentage of TEA businesses with owner/managers who have at least some secondary education.
Competitors	Percentage of TEA businesses started in markets where not many businesses offer the product (i.e., low level of competition).
New products	Percentage of TEA businesses offering products that are new to at least some of their customers.
New technology	Percentage of TEA businesses using technology that is less than five years old.
Gazelle	Percentage of TEA businesses exhibiting high employment expectations (i.e., expecting to have more than 10 employees within five years and representing an increase of 50 percent or more over the current number of employees).
Export	Percentage of the TEA businesses having at least some foreign customers.
Informal investment (mean)	The mean amount of informal investment over the last three years.
Business angel	The percentage of the population aged 18–64 years that provided funds to new businesses in the past three years (excluding stocks and funds).
Informal investment	The amount of informal investment calculated as the product of the previous two variables.

Note: The 19 variables in this table are reduced to 15 in the body of the text. That is because several of the variables presented here are combined to form the measures discussed in the text and illustrated in figure 1.

TEA = total early-stage entrepreneurial activity.

Appendix 2. Description and sources for the institutional variables used in the GEDI

Institutional variable	Description	Source of data
Domestic market	Domestic market size, that is, the sum of gross domestic product plus the value of imports of goods and services, minus the value of exports of goods and services, normalized on a 1–7 scale.	World Economic Forum, Global Competitiveness Index, *Global Competitiveness Report 2012–13*, p. 496
Urbanization	The percentage of the population living in urban areas.	Population Division, United Nations, 2011, http://data.worldbank.org/indicator/SP.URB.TOTL.IN.ZS/countries
Market agglomeration	A combined measure of domestic market size and urbanization, calculated as the product of the two previous variables.	Authors' calculation
Postsecondary education	Gross enrolment ratio in tertiary education, 2011, or latest available data.	UNESCO, http://stats.uis.unesco.org/unesco/TableViewer/tableView.aspx?ReportId=167
Business risk	The business climate rate "assesses the overall business environment quality in a country… It reflects whether corporate financial information is available and reliable, whether the legal system provides fair and efficient creditor protection, and whether a country's institutional framework is favorable to intercompany transactions" (http://www.trading-safely.com/). This variable is a part of the Country Risk Rate. The alphabetical rating is turned to a 7-point Likert scale from 1 ("D" rating) to 7 (A1 rating).	Coface, http://www.coface.com/CofacePortal/COM_en_EN/pages/home/risks_home/business_climate/rating_table?geoarea-country=&crating=&brating=
Internet usage	The number Internet users in a particular country per 100 inhabitants.	International Telecommunication Union, 2012 data, http://www.itu.int/en/ITU-D/Statistics/Pages/stat/default.aspx
Corruption	The Corruption Perceptions Index (CPI) measures the perceived level of public-sector corruption in a country. "The CPI is a survey of surveys based on 13 different expert and business surveys." Overall performance is measured on a 10-point Likert scale.	Transparency International, 2012, http://cpi.transparency.org/cpi2012/results/
Economic freedom	Business freedom is a quantitative measure of the ability to start, operate, and close a business that represents the overall burden of regulation, as well as the efficiency of government in the regulatory process. The business freedom score for each country is a number between 0 and 100, with 100 equaling the freest business environment. The score is based on 10 factors, all weighted equally, using data from the World Bank's *Doing Business* database.	Heritage Foundation, World Bank, http://www.heritage.org/index/explore.aspx
Gender equality	The female economic participation and opportunity subindex is a part of the Gender Gap Index. It has three parts: the participation gap, the remuneration gap, and the advancement gap. The participation gap is captured using the difference in labor force participation rates. The remuneration gap is captured through the ratio of estimated female-to-male earned income. The gap between the advancement of women and men is the ratio of women to men among legislators, senior officials, managers, and technical and professional workers.	World Economic Forum, *Global Gender Gap Report 2012*, pp. 10–11
Absorption of technology	Firm-level technology absorption capability: "Companies in your country are (1 = not able to absorb new technology, 7 = aggressive in absorbing new technology)."	World Economic Forum, *Global Competitiveness Report 2012–13*. p. 489
Staff training	The extent of staff training: "To what extent do companies in your country invest in training and employee development? (1 = hardly at all; 7 = to a great extent)."	World Economic Forum, *Global Competitiveness Report 2012–13*. p. 447

IDENTIFYING THE OBSTACLES TO HIGH-IMPACT ENTREPRENEURSHIP IN LATIN AMERICA AND THE CARIBBEAN

Market dominance	Extent of market dominance: "Corporate activity in your country is (1 = dominated by a few business groups, 7 = spread among many firms)."	World Economic Forum, *Global Competitiveness Report 2012–13*. p. 451
Technology transfer	The innovation index from the Global Competitiveness Index is a complex measure of innovation including investment in research and development by the private sector, the presence of high-quality scientific research institutions, the collaboration in research between universities and industry, and the protection of intellectual property.	World Economic Forum, *Global Competitiveness Report 2012–13*. p. 20
GERD	Gross domestic expenditure on research and development (GERD) as a percentage of GDP, year 2011 or latest available data. Puerto Rico, Dominican Republic, and United Arab Emirates are estimated.	UNESCO, http://stats.uis.unesco.org/unesco/TableViewer/tableView.aspx?ReportId=2656
Business strategy	The ability of companies to pursue distinctive strategies involving differentiated positioning and innovative means of production and service delivery.	World Economic Forum, *Global Competitiveness Report 2012–13*. p. 20
Globalization	A part of the Globalization Index measures the economic dimension of globalization. The variable involves the actual flows of trade, foreign direct investment, portfolio investment, and income payments to foreign nationals, as well as restrictions of hidden import barriers, mean tariff rate, taxes on international trade, and capital account restrictions. Data are from the 2013 report and based on the 2010 survey.	KOF Swiss Economic Institute, 2010; Dreher (2006). http://globalization.kof.ethz.ch/media/filer_public/2013/03/25/rankings_2013.pdf.
Depth of capital market	One of the six subindexes of the Venture Capital and Private Equity Index, this variable is a complex measure of the size and liquidity of the stock market and the intensity of initial public offerings, mergers and acquisitions, and debt and credit market activity. There were some methodological changes over the 2006–12 time period, so comparison with previous years is not perfect.	EMLYON Business School France and IESE Business School, Barcelona; Groh, Liechtenstein and Lieser (2012).